Children of the Anxious City

Al Russell

Children of the Anxious City **©2018** by **Al Russell**. Published in the United States by Vegetarian Alcoholic Press. Not one part of this work may be reproduced in any fashion without expressed written consent from the author. For more information, please contact vegalpress@gmail.com

Grateful Acknowledgements:

"Bloodletting"—*Adanna*, Fall 2013
"What Happened to Rev. Baxter's Son"—*Euphony*, Spring 2014
"Night Music in Five Acts"—*Du Kool*, January 2015
"Diana," "Leda," and "Eurydice"—*So to Speak*, August 2015
"Electric Blanket" and "Music Box"—*MUSH/MUM*, February 2016
"A Story with Lots of Bugs in it Eventually," "Return to Earth," and "Red Sky at Night"—*Outlook Springs*, Fall 2016
"Christ the Redeemer" and "The Virgin Hagiosoritissa"—*Midway*, April 2017
"Age of Light"—*Bop Dead City*, May 2017
"SCREAM"—*Eastern Iowa Review*, October 2017
"Free Association"—*Jersey Devil*, October 2017
"Spawn"—*The Light Ekphrastic*, November 2017
"Overheard at a Bar Near My Home"—*Imitation Fruit*, February 2018
"The Infant in the Rushes"—*The SquawkBack*, July 2018

¿Cómo hablar el no-yó sin dar un grito?

César Vallejo

For Jayce

Contents

Music Box....1
Electric Blanket....2
Diana....3
Mermaids....4
Sonnet for an Anxious Child....5
End-of-the-World Death Machine Sonnet....6
Overheard at a Bar Near My Home....7
Return to Earth....8
Age of Light....9
SCREAM....10
Free Association....11
Christ the Redeemer....12
Leda....13
What Happened to Rev. Baxter's Son....14
Anxieties of the Swamp....15
What Audubon Saw....16
Hookah Parlor, Gas Station....17
A Story with Lots of Bugs in it Eventually....18
Still Life....19
Still Life with Fruit Bowl....20
Rememberton....21
A Weaver's Rebellion: Death....23
Night Music in Five Acts....24
New Season....25
The Tibetan Mastiff Itself....26
Making Hay....27
Landscape....28
Landscape with Rover....29
Spawn....30
The Infant in the Rushes....31
The visible and the tangible are two different things entirely (OR: If the sky's the limit, that still means it's in my fucking way)....32
Smile....33
Sick....37
Bloodletting...38
Burial Site....39
The Virgin Hagiosoritissa....40
Grey Gardens....41
August....42
Circumstances, August....43
Real Pain, Real Penance....44
The Bank Robber....45
Planting Time in Suburbia....46
Hungry for Gods....47
Revenge of the Nerds....48
Plagued by Nightmares....49

Dirge After Chopin....50
Scenes from the End of the World....51
The Lamplighters....52
The Lamplighters Part II: Gaslight....53
The Spirit of the Bee Hive....54
Emaciated Torso....55
Alaskan Glasses....56
This is It....57
Refrain....58
Eurydice....59
Red Sky at Night....60

Music Box

It was very small,
at first. Then, we looked
into it and saw
our mothers' faces
in the gold filigree,
fish-mouthed, weeping
at what we had done.

Then, a wave of tinny violins
overtook us like giant white
naked bats. The kitchen
got smaller and smaller, the sound
got bigger and bigger, music filled the room,
a handful of falling icicles
trickling to a halt—

no more music, then.
It swallowed all our whole
eyes; we were left
unblinking, slicing
carrots mid-chop,
upset buttermilk carton
and bloody fingers.

Electric Blanket
For Mekeel

Do any of us know
the utter loving kindness
of copper wires?
They give such warmth,
ask only in return
that they be coiled up
properly in storage.
People are not
always
like that.

In a fugue state I felt angel mutts licking my sore back with their halos

I giggled, swooned,
hoped, in this moment where all was right,
the house might burn down and the cough drops might choke me to death.

Diana

shot someone today with a rubber suction cup dart in archery class then
trekked red paint footprints like the ten of diamonds five peas to each
diamond all over the top of abe lincoln at mount rushmore my dogs went
with me too sniffed the paint as tho i had real-life shot the guy with a sharp
arrow in the belly then danced around in his blood like making wine i'll admit
i wanted to he was being a real asshole tho abe lincoln's all right by me

Mermaids

Underwater
things look more honest

blurry. Open your eyes
and everything sears them.

This is why the holy rollers do it

this is why they don't fear death

because the second the river hits your scalp
it's like peach pits cracking on the sidewalk
it's like being born.

Sonnet for an Anxious Child

In first grade the other kids pile their jackets
in the corner where too-skinny Jolene is made
to sit. She was chastised no less than three times
today for fidgeting: picking Elmer's Glue off
the bottle top, scratching tape off her name tag on
the desk, peeling paint off the door frame.
Mrs. Bluth with the pink nails yelled,
Mrs. Bluth who is always right. Jolene has
been sitting too long, she itches. She bugs.
Bins of dinosaurs and Mega Blox are not for
her, the straw-headed bean pole would pick
her teeth with the toys' hard edges.
And, "no one likes a Nervous Nelly,"
and her name is Jolene, not Nelly.

End-of-the-World Death Machine Sonnet

Do not just blast it away. We'll need it in
the coming months. Everything
will crumble, ash explosions fluttering
dollar bills from out the molten
sky will be our currency.
Better than this rain. Do not just
chuck it from the wall plug-in, putz
its cord across the room, hissing, canny.
Like an old ham
radio, I'll need it sooner or later,
to see if anyone is still out there
after the gates creak open
and my nostrils fill with head-aching
sea water. I can't swim, not for that long.

Overheard at a Bar Near My Home

"I lost fourteen teeth that day.
Gambling.
Not my teeth.
Other people's."

Notes of this man's voice
make me imagine the gnashers
he could have stolen
had he been better at craps,
musky yellow molars
mushy with bad-apple-brown spots,
incisors chipped down to
points finer than felt-tipped pens.
His opponent, original owner
of the tokens, might could get a new set
with the money he saved
betting his teeth instead.

"I want diamonds, Ben,
flatout diamonds!"

. . . He'd say to the jeweler-dentist,
and happy Ben might saw
into a lump of rock and extract
canines shinier than God's teeth if he has them,
plugging the bloody sockets, dark garnets
dripping down and clotting gingival
around the new choppers.
And did our barroom narrator
get any souvenirs,
playing that poor sap
for his rotting bicuspids?

"He coulda lost the top row easy,
but I just knocked him one good."

The storyteller spits a jagged sparkle
to the bottom of his glass.

Return to Earth

Ask yourself at dawn
how faces can fade from memory easily
as a human body
deteriorates, eaten
by cells multiplying as they feed.
There are people gone
or dead or fucked off somewhere;
thinking of them too hard
is like looking at the sun,
blurs their faces
so you can't see
their long noses, the ways their eyes are set, or hear
their pitchy/resounding voices.
They are blank
skin-colored ovals
who may have said worthwhile things.

Ask their memories
which of those things you might have missed,
but you can't think how they might answer
(crinkling foreheads, *whale...*
before each pause)

then Roger Daltrey's face,
coming up through iron-pinned sand,
struggles to keep
metal grains from its open mouth
and a voice talks at you and says,
"This.
This.
This."

From the ceramics of Koie Ryoji

Age of Light

What did this Venus, with hair like vapor,
what did she think would happen in the mirror?
A terrible combustion: cloudless body
hewn in a plaster mask, cold moon buoyed
out to a people-less, thoughtless ocean
absent of will. She is no more vain
to look at herself than to keep herself
alive by eating, and now there aren't even ashes.

From the photography of Man Ray

SCREAM

In the awful heat that bakes the flesh of the ground into dry red dirt that is et by panting wild dogs, in the awful setting sun the street lights wink on an awful warning. Across, the neighbors' yards are nothing but dust and scurrying animals—squirrels, why squirrels, the squirrels must be sleeping, these are larger, no hair on their feverish bodies, small-dog-size, aquatic paws replaced by hands—HANDS—it can't be right. They are grabbing humanoid, long, squirming tails like monkeys—they are not supposed to be here. This is illegal. They scurry. They swarm. They look over. One forms words with wormy toothless lips, not English, not language, something older, something dead, my own mouth sticks itself in a tight ring, a letter O, a silent howl.

Free Association

Trees: Good.
God: Damn dog. Mad god.
Hell: All Montagues. Especially that one.
Vindication: Of the rights of whoever wants 'em.
Vindictive: Everyone.
Strangers: Your personality is showing, mine is not.
Tension headaches: My face hurts from oversmiling.
Eat: Or don't.
Eye roll: Delicious. Delicacy. Indecent.
Iambic: Inhale slowly, exhale heavy sigh.
Paint: Pointillism.
Rock stars: Always wear capes.
Husband: He's working, he'll get here soon.
Solve for X: Can't be helped.
Chromosomes: Determine fate.
Dress: Flourish of colored perfume.
Boots: Still kick, guard your shins.
South: Compass rose, night blooming jasmine.
Police blotter: Check the airwaves for dead friends.
Free fall: You're a hypnogogic jerk.
Talking: Nonsense through sleepy teeth.
Mother: I'll name her Inconsistent. She'll grow tall as an oak.

Christ the Redeemer
Parque Nacional da Tijuca, Alto da Boa Vista, Rio de Janeiro

When his father's eye opens over him
waxing him in cool light over the river,
even us faithless are stunned.
Whatever happens at last,
I hope he can escape
the old blood staining his robes,
the loneliness no one told him
was part of being human.

Leda

I
My fly's zipper
caught pubic hair
uprooted it
pinched the follicle
wings beat like hooves
punched my chest
beak punctured hymen
oh it was glorious
rough and tumble
and a spatter of blood

I was given a great gift.

*Why do you say it
in such a mocking tone?*

I don't,
at least
not yet.

II
A blue eye, a blue, blue eye, blue for want of brown.
My Castor dropped his spoon, it clattered like magazine fire
(startled me) and now he is a man. I washed Pollux carefully
until he outgrew the sink, the tub, the yard, they are growing, growing (terrifying)
and eclipse my view of the sky, everything now dark blue and too opaque.
They're too big for their forgotten mother, all I have left
are these ostrich egg shells.

*Stupid Leda—
women are only mothers,
wives,
sisters of men.*

That's all right, Zeus. You'll die too.

What Happened to Rev. Baxter's Son

Wet boots, size 16
drag the purple corpse
without struggle up the hill.
"This your boy?"
The badge sparkles. Annie,
7, peeks her strawberry
cheeks and hair,
is shushed back inside.
A note: *To my father*
I leave my mangled body,
a box full of stars.

Anxieties of the Swamp

John is an invalid,
John is a man.

He eats his breakfast sitting up in bed,
draws the spires
of the grand cathedral
outside his window,
delicately watercolors
astutely watched birds
with his small feminine hand
like a delicate blossom,
the rest of him disfigured.
When it storms
John hides under the blankets
with his basset hound because
the thunderclaps sound like bombshells.

John is a pedant,
John has a wooden leg.

John is a racist because his old dog
growls at Black men's faces in the snow.

During the year
when the outside colors change,
John records them all.
He presses his scarred cheek
to the glass pane, sometimes
it feels cold. Other times
he puts his one beautiful limb
(hard to lift as if
of heavy metal) to his breast,
weighing on it
severely and feels his heart
burst through its ribcage.

What Audubon Saw

In the gold-green leaves
of the New Jersey Sumac
there are more than moths
and spiders. The vociferous
goatsucking whippoorwill
lurks on the lichened branches.
The bird seems benign
with its whisker feathers
and widish beak, but what
has terrified children
for thousands of years
is the nightcry shriek,
the rambling cooing refrains
sounding like a man
being beaten to death
for stealing.

Hookah Parlor, Gas Station

Keep to the wall, plaster-flat mouth shrouded in drawn drops of Turin blood, door opens, stone door closes, revisionist. Silent snow under one light pole continents, fantastic centuries away. Affirmative. Why did you kill my dead hair? Answer: it was getting too long. I could plait whole unfeeling feet of it, comb the length of the evening, comb my own light blue streaks into the morning. Eyes perplexed, long, too-synchronous simply hand over small tittering smile, diagetic mime yowls at that fat jaundiced baby, what the hell is wrong with it, near the shaking neon genie bottle, illusion of light, sleight of hand, you think it's dancing across the top of that store front.

A Story with Lots of Bugs in it Eventually
For Charlie

So yes we know our teachers are dying,
and we are dying, our tribes are dwindling,
kids I'm looking at you
giving you these little
bright bulbs to string around
my tomb stone like a barbed wire
but only to blink my spirit
into the dark world rather
than keep things out
or in.

So as I was thinking
this lofty human bullshit
the grubworm came
jiggling like a jazz vibraphone,
heat-seeking missile
stop-motion flopping
toward my molded boot
close in shape and size
to the lovable and noble
roley-poley bug, but a gross
antagonistic daguerreotype
to squish, to retch, to swoon, to kill it. I killed it.

So when I said words are a swarm of black flies
thickening the sick
orange of that street light (as in, that one),
this is what I meant:

Still Life

This dress in a color photograph was made
painstakingly by children's hands
centuries ago. It has a frilled cravat
and matching bonnet, full of holes.
She boils similar articles—
along with her grandnieces' culottes and cardigans,
twin girls playing hobby-horse and jacks—
clothes float like soupy cabbage,
belching with earthen stinks and lye.
The old crone even has a cauldron
over the fire she's made
in the debris-littered mill yard;
the little girls' father, the family's 1st night college man,
reads to them about Scotland, where witches' warts
like their grandaunt's give them magic.
The kettle must weigh 300 lbs. empty
and needs both sons of her sister to lift it,
the cleansing power of poisons
in 100 parts water prune the hands
to soft rumpled linen, blanched as grace
under infernal fire, the steam
presses and oppresses (only fine days
are fit for washing).
She turns away. Mill towns are prone
to stark breezes where fluff
inhabits the lungs. The bubbles release hot gas.
"There, there is your air moving,"
she says.

Still Life with Fruit Bowl

Touching the cloth on the sandy-hued table, I can feel its muslin roughness
against the stained grain's smooth, wooden warmth, coolness and uneven
        stucco
of the earthenware pot, soft lumps under the skins of those French pears.
Just a girl wandering through a room, hands out to feel what my blind mind
knows must be the colors things are.

That cloth must have been in hot grass, the table not made by an electric saw
or belt sander; the wood doesn't smell of light burning. The jar is the sky when
        it's about
to rain, thick and cold on one lung, the pears smell like nothing. That breed no
        longer
exists. All I have to compare (as the blindfold slips off) are other red and
        yellow things
here and now—candycorns, the pears smell of candycorns.

From the painting by Paul Cézanne

Rememberton

Remember, remember, remember
not that you did remember but that
someone had to remind you
it happened so really it's up to them
what you remember them planting

that grew like a dandelion
with its puffy seed umbrellas out
this crack between big gray
stone slabs that are gaps in knowledge

in the first place.
Remember Uncle Adolf
who had nothing
attached to his name
except he was a creepy
pervert that touched your knees
when they got skinned, and laughed?

And that big animal, that's called a giraffe
no it isn't that one
with the legs
that is incorrect,

that quote from a famous
historical figure
the saintly savior who brought all the Africas
together, that's actually the summer's
hit radio single lyrics, and we ought
to bash you over
the head with an oar
and take your calf skin
wallet, you oaf.

Here at Rememberton, town of remembering, the head is a
pig slop trough, and we consider it
our duty to keep it that way
so kindly shut the fuck up
about the facts you think you have, stop screaming
about the smell of fallen leaves,
glimmer of a blue rhinestone jacket, or the way
an old Oldsmobile chugs when it is cranked, because what if
you're wrong and the commotion in the attic
turns out to be *not*
fluttering of batty wings but rather
thousands of clam shells

clickety clacking their agreement
with your decision
to wear pants today.

A Weaver's Rebellion: Death

In a dream I felt an overwhelming sense of dread
like an invisible wolf's skeleton
jabbing at me with its brittle sticks,
claustrophobic sensation of being followed
by someone you can't see but can hear them breathing
or locked in a hot dark box and left to guess
what other consciousnesses, what others, might share it.
You say I've got a short fuse,
but this is how it is every day.
No formidable monsters, no spectres from the past,
no angry antagonisms, only a cat
scratching at my pocket full of garlic powder and thyme,
behind which lies an old, unclear photograph.

From the Etching Triptych by Käthe Kollwitz

Night Music in Five Acts

I
It's just the cold white
of your naked back lumpy
with vertebrae when the moon
comes in. It lights the yard's tree green
from underneath. Show. Explain.

II
And why can't I sleep, oh yeah, that letter
I fear from what feels
like ages ago.
Dumb shit
why didn't I lock the front door?

III
I did put my hand on that head stone.
It glowed eyeless pink when I took my hand away.
I was there
it was night
and it was night.

IV
Who cares
about the war on, the riots,
or what year it is,
we've all been
the shrimp,
the cloud, the boat,
the cormorant, the bebop xylophone, the estuary,
the clown wig. Right?

New Season

Crackpots have discovered
a new way to tell
good circulation:
Hair on the Toes.
But it's summer and my hairy feet
are almost-translucent-white—nude, bone-diseased frozen peas.
In trying to write every love epistle,
the hand slips, the wrist opens, the veins belch
ugly and purple all over the page.

Why so hard, to choke out things we mean?

I call out for you at night.
I live in a tree with big doors,
lumps under the green velvet carpets.
We never knew one another. You just stood there,
hands full of dark sapphires.
Do you have dreams like that too?

The Tibetan Mastiff Itself

My friend Mollie has a blue ceramic fu dog
and a lot of grace, both of which she carries
in her reluctantly shaven armpits.
Her pet's glaze is uneven,
but her poise is plotted and squared,
shows in her forehead's furrows. Deep thought.
The thing she cradles,
silky and vital, has *dog* in the name
but resembles a lion.
It just sits there,
never comes when called.
But I think
if anyone could coax the thing to move
in a voice that even over the phone
you can still tell is coming
from a warmly smiling mouth,
its owner would.

Making Hay
For Bill

Hey do you know the smell
of a free-bleeding seven-year-old's
skinned hand as it mingles
with peaty wet sod from a Southern forest?
It is almost *OXIDIZED COPPER*. I too
had a pastoral childhood
of primo nature-mulched leaves and lonely
dreaming I could be anywhere else
(but indifferent if I was), draped
in some lavender cape
trimmed in ermine, hiding my cellophane
dragonfly wings—nowhere REAL™, you understand,
because I thought the world was not vibrant enough.
 . . . And I ripped the unholy neon-pink-orange
surveying ribbons off skinny trees
 . . . And I heard the roar vibrating the ground
of the race track in the distance
like the blood pounding in my ears,
a wounded animal.

Landscape

Today it looks dark, no sun
all the trees are sickly
from the windows the smell of food

like night, but paraphrased.

Nothing is missing
not a stitch of clothing
or a blade of grass
is out of place.

This is how things are:

Inside the fence
children play ball
on a court choked with weeds,
glass, tire tracks.
Every day they parade
to the big industrial school building.

Every day they come back out.

Wade through rusted
beer bottle caps
to get to the one
hole in the chain-link
a crack in the armor
people cross sometimes
to wound the anxious city.

Landscape with Rover

Stuck inside this glass eye,
this shatter-proof orb,
it means a lot when the wind is gold
with the seeds of dandelions
in a moss-carpeted field.
You have it
then you lose it
and it sounds like a wheeze
when you travel over pastoral scenes
in this subsuming womb. No daffodils,
no children lying down
with docile beasts, only the sound
of the wind in your head, coarse
Aeolian voice of God. How does
your own voice sound? Like too-
big tires flush over gravel? Peepers
high, thick, throaty at midnight?
Clanging? It doesn't matter.
You are free to move, free
to not speak. The dandy
lionseeds puff out and make
their ways and you follow them there.

Spawn

everything smelled of mossy wood
at the stream behind my house
I scooped fistfuls of baked mud

the hollows spoke
of the markings of animals

foxes, bird dogs

but we couldn't find any
so imagined them
chocolate ice cream smeared around your mouth,
grotesque harlequin

and I pretended I had gotten
too much mustard on my clothes to wear them

we took them off
when it rained
I was small but I felt something
sticky between my legs
when I put my toes in the cool wet leaves
my tiny nipples stood erect

I cut my foot
on a sliver of green glass
behind a wall of earth

The Infant in the Rushes

Why
          did the baby water moccasin float in
on a palm-sized river,
flick its tongue to sniff
our toast and bacon,
through the crack between
the foundation and door?
Will it poison us?
It broke the shell of its tiny egg
with one tooth, and now
it can't tell the difference
between floor and ceiling
(when all you see is up,
up's direction matters
only a little). Down the back stairs
the basement flooded again,
water the color of red clay
up to your waist
even after zoos of insects
bounced on the current
out the open hatch.
The water moccasin ate the insects.
He enjoyed them very much.

The visible and the tangible are two different things entirely
(OR: If the sky's the limit, that still means it's in my fucking way)

This big prism in my hands is heavy, full of the weight
of the light universes it contains
you can look into it   (if you want),
                                                but
don't lose your vision
from its bright red and green
beams skittering across your eyelids,
lest you get the gift of second sight.
All these tiny geometric worlds
cities of sharp-toothed mountains, straight lines going
logically from one place to one
more, refract reaching infinite if
you were to see them.

How is something so regimented so full
of ecstatic trilling
an inaudible but abundantly visible
water glass roundly warping the dinner partner across the table
so formal, so bulging overrun. It,
Energy, kept by exceeding Its
container. It's perfectly maddening, you know, like

a brash splatter
of your strawberry icecreamcone
against a mighty oak, when its sweetness
oozes pink into a picture of a hybrid
lobster-android, too real
to be stuck there/
                            or wandering
(flailing its circuitry, its chrome pincers) around
terrorizing joggers
in the park—

Smile

Tongue a wide mushed beefsteak,
yellow ivorychipped teeth
spaced for the black keys,
too many orthodontists
and their incompetent hygienists
smelled my poppyseed breath and tried to cut
the skin flaps in my gums like I was the fucking
Elephant Man.
I am so incredibly proud
to have this fuzzy crooked smile
that spits in their mouths and makes my lips
split even wider, Cheshire moon.

Sick

Day 1
bell peppers and purple smoke
mouse corpses
littering the linens
what terrifying masks
you saw in the night
cyclorama of a motorcycle at high speeds
the trees were whisked faces
snapped at you
as you drove past
however coarsely woven
basket cases
of the mumps

Day 2
lying paralyzed
in a wakeful body
a thing *like* sleep

electrical currents
pass through eternally
it hurts
must jump out
of this skin like a sausage casing
meagerly destitutely starving spelless feckless
trembles

Day 3
the apples
have fallen
they bruised bouncing
down the stairs
and the mayor
of the city of Hippocampus
has ordered a decree

a vow of silence signed in blood

Day 4
like so many
(few) tin spoons
sideways in the drawer
fingers interlace like fork tines
stop
being so mocking
with your ability to sleep

balls of phlegm-
choked light
Christmas tree bulbs
push
down veins and tendons
signals
across the wire
dumb thick-tongued mind
taste-samples little
everything can be considered
at least thirteen ways
I'm coming
to understand
someone's knees are in my chest

Day 5
how is it that when sleeping
or not sleeping
you have the power of thinking
of absolutely nothing
till daybreak till
it's time to put on the sun's hat
and join everyone
the neighbors on the porch
mentioning you're starting up earlier
than usual and what a nice new pattern
"no"
you say
"I never went to sleep"

Day 6
I hear my lungs heave back and forth
filling deflating
thick rubber bags
(full of I hope not fluid
never fluid
or choked-up dry
rice grains caught in the throat
inhaled then
legs splayed and immovable
dove-like).

Day 7
defecate and open your nose
your sensitive palate yes
yes now more now more
stiff bowels
rigid tubes

of skin and so much blood
not *your* blood *my* blood
the wrong blood
in the muck of an opened shitpail
we'll make you one of us yet

Day 8
ghost of my father
sits in the figurine
bores holes with its glass eyes
through the darkness
sprung back hair bristles
static
I look down
three feet at your head (my head?)
we pop open our eyes
and the last two weeks
come leaping out

Day 9
it is easy to feel brilliant when no one is listening
beautiful when no one is looking
eloquent with a raked throat
fever dream in a night desert
alive but motionless weightless
in dead space

Day 10
Just like a shark with its eyes and rows of teeth if you stop moving stay sedentary don't float around from place to place
bed couch kitchen table room to room middle of the street across the continent you will cease to be
so if I stop writing I will stop thinking about breathing never start breathing again
and if I go to sleep I have to make sure I don't wake because I will never sleep again
never wake from sleep again never wake up

Day 11
the plants
they've stopped their buds
stopped growing
they may stir
restless
again
but now lie fallow in frost-hardened soil
we grow and grow
and grow aching our hands toward the sun

until we shrink from it
and begin to die

Bloodletting

Sorry my love,
I was mending
one of your shirts,
the yellow one,
and I know
the splatter looks
like a drop of mascara
from a weepy eye—
it is only
where I pricked my finger
and stupidly let blood spill.

Burial Site

"Here in Hell,
there are no birds,"
You say as though
you expect a big
reaction.
I mean.
You're right.
Dead silence.

All these statues,
who are they?
This used to be a whole city I hear
but the past is past.
Were they all this size?
The birds, I mean,
big birds,
big as gods,
big old monsters

who read their laws from stone
obelisks around this feeding pit
littered with humanoid skulls? I imagine pterylas
spread like a tarp, tiny maroon plumes peppered
with cyan, sprinkled with forest green, getting aged
as the Dickens,
big birds,
big as gods,
big old monsters
used to live here and shriek out over
the distant lakes resounding. What wasted life.

The Virgin Hagiosoritissa

Mary's puffy crow's feet
have been crying about the world
again, she misled us all.
How in the hell
did that painter jot her down so fast,
before she could get her makeup on
like normal?
I've seen those Hollywood epics
with their false street preachers rubbed in bone dust
on every damned corner,
I've seen their ladies with the lovely hair
all done up—the quiet,
rosacea'd one smiling moronically at God
with clean, clear eyes is not Mary. These are Mary's
glum dark bleary eyes like unfortunate
sky-cataracts, her filthy horned hands.

(*Cyprus Icon*)

Grey Gardens
"You don't see me as I see myself, but it's very good, what you see me as."
—Little Edie

I
Once
I lit a strand of
my hair on fire
just to smell it—as
white as white as white, as
each time I look in the mirror
I hear my rail-thin
mother's voice complain
of her fat, the bags
under her eyes, so
are they mine (makes me not want to age)? Who cares, I won't
have anyone to give
me large green jewels, pearls
big as oranges,
to give one's life
to a man/or one's mother, old abandoned
barn full of smells—pine straw, leather, so much horseshit—

II
What's all this
blackish metal under my nails?
. . . Never so deeply
felt the wound
of an unfamiliar woman's bitter rind,
teeth ground so tight
the jaws push one
another out her head, my wet
toast heart got too spongy to beat
like normal.
That face that face it don't
stop growing, the more I look at it the more I think
of it, vomit out a grossly
misshapen cantaloupe.

III
one a faded Day-Glo velvet poster folds itself into the dust of a moth's wings,
two a sunspot looking all like the face of Jesus,
three a Whirling Dervish in the midst of a hundred thousand paper flags,
finally
the intoxicating scent
of burning hair.

August
Elegy for Varga Girls

Of course it's lazy in August, of course it's hot,
look at my eyes, and tell me if you think they mind.
I'd rather be doing anything than nothing, rather nothing
than anything else. Tasting sour persimmons on just
the tip of my tongue, my nostrils fill (like falling
up not down) with a smell like burning sage, like roasting brown
tree nuts the size of a knock on the chin.
How bewildering, this white, getting good
and sickly white, then sitting there for hours in the sun
doing nothing, getting browner, and not pinker, and not able
to stay this milky color, color of the taste
of the flaps of envelopes.

Circumstances, August
For my thirtieth birthday

Perseids formed
           impermeable
gemstone
—after all
aren't diamonds just

hard carbon

polished manticore

auroch shit?

Hiking Black Mountain
midsummer a week
from labor's
not
easy. Radical. Thanks.

O Creeley's ghost
I invoke thee   bless the belly
of the
mother of
a child who   is
capable of making a sound—more
at least
than a
breathless
nightmare
gasp
—next time

Real Pain, Real Penance

I have a cheek within my cheek,
iron-coated and dismal.
The pinging sensation of biting a peppercorn sends an alert like a ball-bearing
zings a horrid clang in the jaw.
Nonceduncecapped in suspicion and fantasy
is how I'd describe myself, and you, and you
and standing here on the edge
of a volcanic lip all I can do is kick
the ball-bearings absentmindedly in and wait
for them to jump back and surf the slow hot honey,
steaming magma
(steaming bullshit)
laughing in schadenfreude as if from outside and above
my own
painful cheek

The Bank Robber

They ran out of my favorite
blue ballpoint pens
at the bank today.
I can't steal them anymore.
Where else will I get them?

Any excuse to go in:
the crisp smell
of fresh ink on paper,
the biscuits for my dog
and lollipops for my nephews,
the jingle of the chains
attaching the harder-to-come-by red pens.

And of course, every time I go
through the revolving door
I can pretend I have money.
But now they're out of my favorite
blue ballpoint pens
I can't pretend anymore.

Planting Time in Suburbia
For Stuart

In a house built in the fifties, on a potholed street
a man lives on treacherous plywood planks.
He asks no joy or anguish from anyone,
but offers quasars in a shrug or wink.

He puts hot rocks on his chest
to keep him breathing properly.
Inside the hovel of his impish skull
no energy is wasted on despair.

Drink from his plastic tea cup,
sit in the sedan he carries,
take note of everything he says and does.

This is not allegory.
This man is no actor.
This is real life.

Hungry for Gods
For Yusef Komunyakaa

I'll bet you used to feel this human too,
once. Now you're surrounded
and you can't go wrong—
the poor girl next to you
quaking with admiration
still feels foreign, yeah?
I'll bet you used to be an unsure kid
overwhelmed to meet,
say, Gwen Brooks, or whoever was around
not yet convinced of your power with words
your mother must have told you about
making images as if
you were throwing pepper into a soup
(my own poem reeks of rhetoricity like green onions).
It must fill your stomach with stones
to be fawned over just because of your name
which sounds like birds at dawn.

Revenge of the Nerds
From Harvey Pekar/Bill Knapp

So what were these nerds like? How wouldya describe 'em?

Glasses, elocution of a thick and mangled accent, hair or lack of hair matted however (straight or curly) is not *hip*, brittle old jazz 45 collectors, doll-stuffing making waifs, Twinkie gobbling fans of Jewish magical realism, sweaty with turmeric, grunting, proud proletariat, hoarders of African masks, Cat People, pork brain subsisters, low-lifed and pimply, intellectuals whose only education is reading, head scratchers, toe tappers, my friend Eric, bus riders, tinkerers, people with gas stoves, wearing tee shirts and too-high pants, socks rolled down around their ankles, their grandfathered houses need work on the plumbing and gutters, a few of them are gay, various prized copies of Moby Dick and worry about super-PACs, buying dried mango and red seedless grapes when they can get them and don't have great dental plans or much luck in love and they are all here, there, everywhere, and this is America.

Plagued by Nightmares

I paid seven dollars
for this cheap gold bracelet
turning my wrist blue,
likeness of a vein
running my arm's circumference.
The rest of the skin clashes,
thin and yellow as an old
lace wedding gown. I'm feeble,
my bones are full of holes,
even at eighty-nine
I'm still plagued by nightmares.
The moon, green as a grape,
as round, as full, as waxy,
reveals a startling, wide
aperture in the dark
hand mirror—my whole face.
It is terrifying.
I turn my attention
to a glass on the night stand,
it slops over the rim, brims
with what looks like brown paint
and milk of magnesia
(though I pine for hemlock,
bitter as corn liquor,
sweet as a jug
of peach brandy).

Dirge After Chopin

They go in   they come out   they go in   they come out

Smoke and blaze   both banks   across the river   bread factory orange

Weld bolts   spark up   hit your face   they go in

They come out   wear a mask   in the gavel   rubble belch

Deep hole   barbed shack   bullet belt   where's your God

They all say: FUCK YOU   GET FUCKED   DON'T LOOK BEHIND

And a soft seep through the warm spongy pores of the bread that has been made into god-consciousness. We're all just peachy here. Simple folk, though whipped. Whupped. Licked
off an ice cream spoon. You go in, you come out. I go in, I come out.
It is boring here. I am full.

TROMP   TROMP   TROMP   TROMP

Big boots   road grind

Here we go anyways   going in and coming out

Scenes from the End of the World

The tickle of an ant on a leg.
The sky, pink and purple-gray.
Someone somewhere
is swallowing a dry avocado pit
the size of an infant fist.

The Lamplighters

Weak, blue filament starts at five,
gets stronger.
It expands. Soon it is the only thing
burning.
It used to be someone's job, in big cities
men complained
that machinery would soon replace them.
They were right—
The lamplighters' kerosene-dipped
rags have puckered
into a foul-smelling ghost that shivers
in the nervous
pixie body between the plexiglass of
then and now,
grubby paw-prints all over it.
When the world
gets very dark I'm glad we won't
need them,
the lamplighters, anymore; I'm afraid
they'd ask me
to be one, no skill or effort required
for this menial
burden, and I'd have to decline.
I'm partial to the blue the night sky gets.

The Lamplighters Part II: Gaslight

In the night   (*it's not night*)
        you hear
children playing   (*or dogs barking*)
        and then
a bleat like a lamb being slaughtered makes you freeze.
                (*Why did you think it was that?*)
You haven't been near a farm   (*except that once*).
A grade school field trip,
the teacher started singing loudly   (*to drown out another kid crying*).
A movie?
                (*There are no movies like that.*)
But your gut said, "a lamb is being slaughtered
                (*a sound you've never heard*)."

You pick up some smeary red clay older,
colder than civilization itself and begin
to stuff it in your mouth.

The Spirit of the Bee Hive

The skin around my scalp woke itchy and warm
less like flesh and more like raw meat
some fetus ate, a larval bee fetus,
as it and they all pulse around the head,
suffocating, of the invading wasp,
twice the size, the cold, the calculating
relentless stinger of a Tommy gun,
they swarm around the hive, swarm, swarm
each hexagonal hole filling with sweet
sticky tears of mustard gas through eyes
like beveled crystal from the cabinet's face
its face like an unholy gas mask, god,
and big, oppressive, badly drawn, boring
burning holes through seared and splintering wood

Emaciated Torso

A woman, sticky with pitch,
brittle thin arms and pine cone hands

in the parking garage's
subterranean yellow,
I thought she was a legless dummy
someone had just dropped off
to forget about. I couldn't
just leave her there.

As I approached
carefully with my comb,
I found a rolled
curlicue of parchment
in the fey thicket of her top shock.
DON'T CHANGE
the scroll's block script said

to whom? I didn't intend to.
I lifted the lady's remnants
amid her still-breathing grunts
of thanks. Despite her thinness
she was heavy as a bag of sand.

Alaskan Glasses

Slits, drilled
into a whale's rib bone
help you see through
the outside
the snow
so bright
you think
your body is dying.
How myopic
to fish through the ice
to inhabit a tarp, to see
only a sliver
of world
with this
artifact, a sliver
thin as
a taut string
you have to walk across
to get
to the rest.

This is It

Lived in a tree,
a wooden crate, a fruit stand,
a garbage pail, love did.
Love calls on the
is it telephone
as you sink your teeth
into the flesh
of a grainy rotting pear
from the place where love
resided once and so did you.
Will you let love
wash you in its
quaking green
under the false
street lamp?
The light comes in
Morse-code-ticks:
Have/
a/
heart./
Don't/
look/
at/
me/
any/
closer.

Refrain

I keep having these obsessive thoughts,
bunch of men sitting around:

Tsar Bomba
Tsar Bomba
Tsar Bomba

little white island infested with sea lice
you're holding the map the wrong way

Tsar Bomba
Tsar Bomba
Tsar Bomba

how many missiles do you think I have,
think I have in my hand?
How many fingers am I holding up
behind my back? Blue card or red?
Eruption of raucous laughter
and fluttering pages make a fast ZZZZZ

Tsar Bomba
Tsar Bomba
Tsar Bomba and Jesus,
Three Stooges-two-fingered points at his eyes,
then mine, then his nail wounds,
and is my schnoz French enough for you
and *Tsar Bomba Tsar Bomba*
my name is Tsar Bomba my name
is Antonia and I wind the wind

Tsar Bomba
Tsar Bomba
Tsar Bomba a black-
-clad man swings a thurible
smoking pendulum winking eyes
like a metronome and an intent cat
and Tsar Bomba and hate, hate, hate, hate
and love, love, love, love.

Eurydice

Last night you were
in danger of rolling off the edge
of the bed, which is very uncommon,
usually you're hogging my side.
You were in danger of rolling off the edge
of the world, into some abyss.
No amount of yelling
or trying to roll you
limp like a big full sack back over
brought you from the crater's lip,
the crater that was nothing. It was only
when I said the word *no*.
softly and held out my hand—do you remember—?
that you took it and nuzzled safe
back to me.
It was
as simple
as that.
Would you
have done
the same?
Are we
the same?
Are you
there?

Red Sky at Night

Some moons
look different.
Some are more green.
Some almost make a sound.

I sat on top of a rock
and looked over, all I could see
was darkness.

But I could hear the ground heaving
and that is what I wanted,

to lie flat on it and let it be under me.

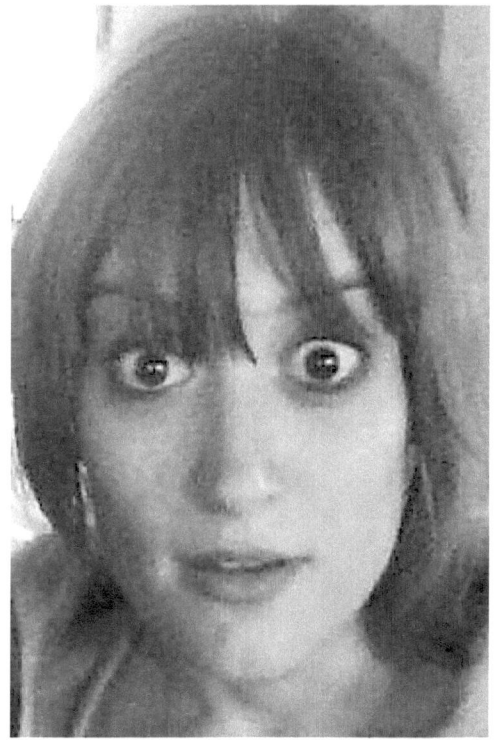

Al Russell is a graduate of the MFA program at the University of New Hampshire. She is a poetry editor at Outlook Springs literary journal. She is also an ordained minister of the Church of the Subgenius. She lives in North Carolina.